ANNA ROSS

Stewart County Outdoor Recreation

A local gal's guide for all the best campgrounds, parks, and boat ramps in Stewart County, Tennessee.

Copyright © 2023 by Anna Ross

All rights reserved. No part of this publication may be reproduced, stored or transmitted in any form or by any means, electronic, mechanical, photocopying, recording, scanning, or otherwise without written permission from the publisher. It is illegal to copy this book, post it to a website, or distribute it by any other means without permission.

Anna Ross asserts the moral right to be identified as the author of this work.

Anna Ross has no responsibility for the persistence or accuracy of URLs for external or third-party Internet Websites referred to in this publication and does not guarantee that any content on such Websites is, or will remain, accurate or appropriate.

Designations used by companies to distinguish their products are often claimed as trademarks. All brand names and product names used in this book and on its cover are trade names, service marks, trademarks and registered trademarks of their respective owners. The publishers and the book are not associated with any product or vendor mentioned in this book. None of the companies referenced within the book have endorsed the book.

First edition

This book was professionally typeset on Reedsy.
Find out more at reedsy.com

Contents

Introduction	1
Campgrounds	3
Parks	19
Boat Ramps/Swimming Holes	27
Conclusion	32
Resources	33

Introduction

*S*tewart County, TN is one of Middle Tennessee's most perfect little hidden gems! Tucked away in a multitude of hills and 'hollers', are some of the most unique, relaxing, and enjoyable places on earth. Please allow me, a Stewart County local gal of 28 years, to enlighten you on some of our town's well-known, as well as not-so-well-known, campgrounds, parks and boat ramps, that are sure to suit any and all of your outdoorsy needs.

This book is one of many books to come, showcasing all the wondrous places our quaint little town has to offer. From primitive camping in the woods, to campgrounds with full RV hook-ups, you are sure to find what you are looking for with your outdoor experience, in this series of outdoor recreation travel guides.

Stewart County is a beautiful oasis, surrounded by plentiful forests, enchanting lakes and ever-flowing rivers and creeks. Are you looking for a place to escape the hustle and bustle of life? Maybe just a place to disconnect and get a feel of "yesteryear"? Give yourself the opportunity to let go of all your worries, and soak in the natural beauty that this area has to offer.

There is absolutely no shortage of divine places to put in a boat, kayak or canoe, nor a lack of waterways for fishing or swimming. This small hometown is bursting with wildlife encounters at nearly every turn, so come visit and witness the bountiful herds of deer in the corn fields, our wild bunnies scurrying about, and if you're really lucky, you might just see one of many majestic bald eagles that reside here, soaring across the sky!

To make this small hometown even more enticing to visit, Stewart County happens to be home to two amazing, history-rich national parks. Fort Donelson National Battlefield will provide you with hours of education and enjoyment, and you'll never run out of trails to trek in Land Between the Lakes. Have no doubt, if a total-outdoors, nature rich vacation is what you're seeking, there's absolutely no better place than this two-stoplight town!

Campgrounds

[**Note:** *Primitive camping is camping in remote areas without amenities like bathrooms, picnic tables, trash cans, or any other man-made structures.*
  All pricing listed reflects pricing found online and should only be considered as an example. Please use the contact information provided before counting on a specific price.]

Piney Campground:

Land Between the Lakes's (LBL) Piney Campground is by FAR the most sought after summer spot in Stewart County. It even has its own Facebook community (Piney Campground @ LBL). With an offering of 384 well established lakefront and wooded sites, 283 of those offering electric and 44 offering sewer, electric AND water, it's no wonder Piney is the place to be! If you're a hardcore outdoorsman who prefers more primitive camping, there is also the option of 57 campsites specifically designated for tent camping, too.

Don't have a camper? Don't want to pitch a tent? NO PROBLEM! This campground also has 19 PRIMITIVE cabins available to rent by the night. They offer nine cabins that sleep four people and 10 cabins that sleep eight. Please note again that these are PRIMITIVE cabins, not luxury cabins. Each cabin comes with beds, and a few bare necessities- like foldable tables and chairs, portable heat and air- this is a NO FRILLS cabin. You can find more information on these primitive cabins on the LBL website listed below.

Having an impressive amount of campsites isn't the only perk this five-star campground has to offer! Piney Campground luxuries also include a beautiful sandy swim beach, playground equipment for the kids, a ball field, archery range, and a campfire theater.

I know by now you're thinking "How could this place get any cooler?"

But, WAIT!! There's more! Piney also has access to trails for biking and hiking, a fishing pier, and not one, but 2 boat ramps for all your water-toy launching needs. This vacation spot is your one-stop shop to keep the entire family entertained all vacation long. There's something for everyone, and this place is also known for hosting all sorts of events for their visitors.

And speaking of SHOP- This campground also has an Outpost open from March through November that sells a lot of those much needed amenities you forgot to grab when you left home.

This campground has multiple bathhouses complete with showers, and a place to do your laundry, too.

- **Address:** 621 Fort Henry Road, Dover TN 37058
- **Phone Number:** 931-232-5331
- **Website:** https://landbetweenthelakes.us/seendo/camping/piney-campground/

Whispering Pines Campground and Cabins:

While Whispering Pines Campground is much smaller than Piney, there is a lot to be said about this quiet, shaded, family-owned little place. This campground holds its own with a 4.1 star rating on google. Top reviewer comments let on that the owner is friendly and happy to offer good advice about local foods, sight-seeing, etc; and many other reviews made mention of this place being peaceful and private.

Overnight stay options for this campground include five small cabins, each that include its own private bath, kitchenette, cable TV, as well as heating and air conditioning. In addition to these cabins, Whispering Pines has a total of 15 RV sites w/ hook-ups, and a limited number of primitive sites for tent campers. This location's open season runs from March through January 15th.

This campground is listed as pet and kid friendly, and includes a small playground for children.

Being located right off the main highway of Donelson parkway, this location might be desirable for hunters and fisherman who are traveling to the area for tournaments, and don't want to stray far from the center of town. They also offer boat parking options with electricity.

Visitors to this campground note that it is a very affordable, no frills place to stay. There is a small store on the property with some limited essentials for sale. It is also noted that this location may not be ideal for "big rigs" over 45 ft in length, due to a few narrow or sharp curves and tree overgrowth.

STEWART COUNTY OUTDOOR RECREATION

- **Address:** 2168 Donelson Parkway, Dover TN 37058
- **Phone Number:** 931-232-4570
- **Website:** facebook.com/whisperingpinesDoverTN
- **Max Stay:** 21 nights

LBL's Gatlin Point:

If primitive camping is how you roll, Gatlin Point, with 11 self-service campgrounds in Land Between the Lakes, may just be the place for you.

The amenities for this camp area are extremely limited, but include a fire pit and bench for each site. There are absolutely NO hook-ups for RVs, nor any source for potable water. If you camp here, you will need to come prepared with your own clean water or resources to make nearby lake water safe for use.

The only other notable conveniences located at this camp is a dumpster for trash, and a vault/pit toilet. *Please note that a pit toilet is exactly how it sounds- an outhouse with a literal hole in the ground for using the restroom; this is not to be confused as a porta-potty, that gets emptied and has chemicals in the bottom.

This location includes 20 first come, first serve campsites, and costs $10 per night. The camp sites are described by others as being decent in size, mostly shaded, with little privacy. There is a small access shore to the lake. It is also important to note that cell service may be questionable at best.

This area is suitable for swimming, kayaking or boating, and includes an accessible boat ramp. Some online reviews mention rough terrain/

unmaintained gravel road, which may not be safe for low-to-the-ground cars. Enter with caution!

- **Address:** Forest Service Road 229 (LBL), Dover TN 37058
- **Phone number:** 270-924-2000/ 800-525-7077
- **Website:** https://landbetweenthelakes.us/seendo/camping/basic/
- **Max Stay:** 14 days

Bumpus Mills Campground:

This well-kept campground is certainly under-rated. It is actually the location I am most familiar with, as this is the place I grew up spending my summers at! Located in the tiny little town of Bumpus Mills, not far from the KY state line, this camping area is a wonderful place for families to spend some down-time in nature.

Operated by the U.S. Corps of Engineers, this location is an excellent place to stay for boating, hiking, fishing, and swimming. There is a nice sandy beach with some benches near the water, as well as multiple concrete picnic tables with grills nearby for families to enjoy their summer days grilling out at the lake!

The road to this summer get-away is paved and easy to navigate, and the camp includes 15 campsites with 30 & 50 amp hook-ups. While there is no sewage to utilize, they do have a nice dump station on the other side of the grounds. The camping sites are gravel, fairly level, and can be utilized for tent camping or campers. They are pull-through sites, ideal for big RVs. This location offers clean shower houses as well as a place to do laundry. Over half of the campsites have views of the breath-taking

Lake Barkley.

This is a pet and kid friendly location. There is a small hiking trail that leads from the camp areas to the swim beach, and if you're lucky, you might see the bald eagles (that live nearby) along your walk. Not far from the swimming area, you'll find a boat ramp for launching, as well as a small fishing dock. The parking lot is big, flat, paved and spacious, allowing plenty of room for large vehicles, trailers, etc. This location would also be a good one to take your kayaks or paddle boats with.

- **Address:** 764 Forest Trail, Bumpus Mills, TN 37028
- **Phone number:** 931-232-8831
- **Website:** https://www.recreation.gov/camping/campgrounds/232537

Bumpus Marina:

Bumpus Marina has gotten a re-vamp and new owner in the more recent years, and is ready to be THE hippest spot on Lake Barkley. This campground and marina has a little bit of everything, and provides ample amounts of entertainment on the summer weekends.

Lodging options include two 4 person cabins, consisting of two bedrooms, as well as a living room, fully equipped kitchen, and full bathroom. These home-away-from-homes are adorable, and also include a flat screen TV in the living room as well as high-speed internet to boot! *Note: These cabins require a two night minimum stay, and cost an average of $129-200 per night, depending on the season.

This location offers 30 amp RV camping (1-7 night rental options), costing roughly $50-75/per night. You must be 25 or older to rent an RV site. Dumping facilities are located at the adjacent campground (Bumpus Mills Campground- 764 Forest Trail)

Now let's get into the fun stuff!

To make the most of your vacation, take advantage of the kayak and paddleboard rentals available: $60 for all day or $40 for a half day rental. What's that? Paddle boats for the kids you say? YES! You can rent those,too. $25 per 2 hrs, with 2-8 hour options! This is also a great place for covered and uncovered boat slip rentals. Speaking of boats, want to take your friends out on a pontoon but don't own one? Yep, you can even rent one of those.

While the Marina's open season is from May through September, their boat ramp access is available year round! Also available only from May-September is their restaurant: Mermaids at Bumpus. This eatery offers classics like burgers, pizza, and hot dogs. They also have pulled bbq nachos or garden fresh salad.

If you're wanting the best of both worlds, Bumpus Marina is going to be your go-to spot. You can enjoy the wonders of nature, spend time out on the gorgeous lake, while still enjoying the energy of great people, awesome music, and good times all around!

- **Address:** 197 Bumpus Mills Marina Road, Bumpus Mills, TN 37028
- **Phone Number:** 931-232-5238
- **Website:** https://bumpusmarina.com/

Brownfield Riverside Resort (and Miss Kay's Country Store):

This resort is another HOT spot by the water, only this one is located in Dover, TN, closer to Paris Landing and LBL. This area's local waterways include the TN river and KY lake.

Brownfield Resort has two lodging options available: Efficiency cabins that sleep four people, and cost $115 per night ($150 deposit), or Mobile homes that sleep seven to eight people, and cost $180 per night ($300 deposit). These both require a minimum of two nights booked. Additionally, they offer leased lots for RVs, that include water, sewage and electric hook-ups.

Patrons of this resort get the luxury of utilizing their outdoor pool! The pool is in a fenced area and includes patio tables, chairs and umbrellas. There is also a small playground area, and access/views of the lake within sight of the cabins and pool area.

But guess what? The pool isn't even the best part. Be sure to check out Miss Kay's Country Store and Nutcracker Shed for a real good time! This place has a full size stage for entertainment, a dance floor, an area to play corn hole, and plenty of big screen TVs to watch all your favorite sports games. This place is known for having karaoke nights, and claims to have "one of the biggest beverage coolers in the area!", making this the perfect weekend fun spot to unwind after a long day on the lake. Or heck, any other day, too!

This excellent facility also has a YEAR ROUND kitchen, ensuring their guests can get fresh hot meals, all year long. And their great stock of commonly needed supplies saves you from having to make a 20 minute trip back into town for any small items you may end up needing.

- **Address:** 960 Brownsfield Road, Dover, TN 37058
- **Phone Number:** 931-305-6064
- **Website:** https://www.brownfieldriversideresort.com/

Elk Harbor Lakeside Campground:

Tucked away in yet another part of Stewart County's vastness lies Elk Harbor, on the banks of the Elk Reservoir in Cumberland City. This campground "sits in the middle of a sportsman's paradise" in Cross Creeks National Wildlife Refuge, consisting of 8,862 acres of open water, woodland, cropland and marsh that support an abundant wildlife population.

This excellent park offers 55 campsites, all offering full hook-ups, picnic tables, and fire rings; all on large, level sites. Shower houses and laundry facilities are available for tenant use. There is a general store as well as a cafe that is open for three meals a day, year round. Some foods offered include burgers, fries, and chicken tenders; as well as all your staple country breakfast meals.

Fun extras you can find at Elk Harbor include picnic and play areas, as well as the ability to rent kayaks and canoes. This area is also great for fishing, boating, bird watching, and a few hiking options too. This campground also offers entertainment such as music and karaoke.

30 amp RV sites are $40 / night and 50 amp sites are $45 / night. Tent sites are priced at an affordable $20 per night. They do offer discounted monthly rates for RV tenants.

- **Address:** 1572 Cumberland City Road, Cumberland City, TN 37050
- **Phone Number:** 931-827-4096
- **Website:** https://elkharbor.com/

LBL's Boswell Landing:

Boswell's Landing is in a dispersed area in LBL, located in somewhat close proximity to Piney Campground. This secluded camp area is a first come, first serve, self-service campground like Gatlin Point. Most of these campsites are located on the edge of the water, with awe-inspiring views. There is a boat dock and as well a ramp for boat launching. This campground's only restroom is a vault toilet. There is a provided dumpster for camper trash.

You'll find plenty of areas to take a dip in the lake, and several picnic tables and barbeque grills for camper use. Make sure to check out some of the hiking and biking trails nearby for some memorable outdoor adventures.

This is a local favorite, and one that will get booked up quickly during busy weekends, especially Memorial and Labor day weekends. It is highly rated on google, and is said to be one of the best backcountry campgrounds of all the 11 dispersed sites in LBL.

Boswell Landing offers 19 spacious campsites that are pull through sites suitable for RVs, campers, or tents as well.

- **Address:** Forest Route 332 in LBL
- **Phone Number:** 270-924-2000

- **Website:** https://thedyrt.com/camping/tennessee/tennessee-boswell-landing

Fat Daddy's Lakeside Tiki Bar & Grill:

Fat Daddy's Lakeside Tiki Bar & Grill is another hot spot that offers ample summertime entertainment. If you're looking for a cold drink and good music, you're sure to find it here.

While they do not offer tent camping sites, they do have RV hook-up sites as well as boat slip rentals available.It is suggested online that this place is suitable for 40 ft RVs and under, due to a tight bridge and sharp turn. There is a boat ramp on site, and a sprinkler area for pets and kids to cool off.

This location is a great spot to visit if you're out cruising the lake in a boat; Stop by to enjoy some good food and awesome live entertainment. They also have corn hole boards available, and the option to buy turtle food to feed those cute little guys off the sides of the floating bar. This place also has a gift shop to purchase t-shirts and other lake related merch!

- **Address:** 119 Driftwood Shores Rd, Dover, TN 37058
- **Phone Number:** 931-232-2243
- **Website:** fatdaddysfun.com

Brand'N Iron Hills:

If you are into ATV off-road adventures, this may just be the spot for you. This location just opened up for reservations in January, and will continue to see growth in the coming years. Locally owned by entrepreneurs, this 40 acre outdoor haven is the perfect choice for seclusion and solitude.

Conveniently located five miles from Barkley Lake and the Cumberland river, this area is the perfect spot to have peace and quiet, while also not being too far from the middle of town. Brand'n Iron Hills has an archery range available for use (bring your own bow), and has a freshwater stream that flows year round, that is a lovely place for little ones to splash and cool off. Most areas of this stream are no deeper than ankle to hip, making it a great and safe place for kids.

The property is split by a 2 lane road, with 7 acres to the North and the other 33 acres to the South. The smaller side is mostly flat, with many trails and a running creek, with a gravel road.

If you're down to adventure into the forest, make sure to have your hiking boots handy! The southern side of this property offers a mature hardwood forest of giant oak trees, and there's a few hills to climb through the trails. There are 3 hills that form a valley in the center, and there you'll find another freshwater stream. This valley was once home to a 1700s settlement, so if you look around, you might just discover some cool old artifacts! The owners of the property encourage you to check things out, but ask that you please leave anything you find where it was, so that others who visit may be able to enjoy those discoveries, too. Main trails are marked clearly with large reflectors for safety.

The campsites offered on this property are very primitive (see above description), and offer no electric or water hook-ups. They do however have large steel fire pits for every site, and you are encouraged to bring your own firewood and have a campfire. Have a hammock? Bring that, too! There are plenty of places around the property to hang a hammock and enjoy the scenery. They also offer clean composting toilets and a locking gate at night for your security.

There are currently 2 campsites available, a creekside site that advertises being able to sleep six, and can accommodate vehicles 30 ft and smaller. Average price to rent this site is $40/night. The second campsite is named "Southern Pine", and this site is able to accommodate up to 15 people, for either tent camping or RVs under 30 ft. The average price for this site is $45/ night for up to 10 people. These sites are located quite a ways from each other, allowing for excellent privacy.

- **Address:** 1249 LongCreek Rd, Dover, TN 37058
- **Website:** https://tinyurl.com/4r93hcx5

(You can also simply go to hipcamp.com and search "Brand n Iron Hills" in Dover TN.)

 *There is currently no phone number or actual website for this camp, as this property is still in its infancy and will be seeing many additions/changes in the future!

Dixieland Cabins & Campground:

This location is a great place to stay for family reunions, events, or just to get away. While Dixieland is located right off the main highway in Dover, the cabins and camping areas are nestled cozily near the woods to provide an excellent outdoor experience while giving you all the conveniences of being in town.

Aside from the full hook-up RV sites available, Dixieland also has five different cabins to choose from. There is a spacious two bedroom cabin with a living room, kitchen and 1.5 baths, two 1 room cabins, and two 2-room cabins. Each smaller cabin has a small kitchen area and bathroom. These cabins range from $100- $150 / night. Additionally, this location offers a two room suite that also has a kitchen area and bathroom for convenience.

This property is conveniently located near KY lake and lake Barkley and is in close proximity to LBL, Fort Donelson, and Paris landing. They have a bath house, laundry room, and offer wireless internet and TV as well.

You can find porch swings and rockers to enjoy on the Lodge porch, there is ample parking for boats, and they also offer a pavilion that can be used for events that includes a large gas grill, serving table and plenty of seating!

- **Address:** 1613 Donelson Parkway, Dover, TN 37058
- **Phone Number:** 931-232-9225
- **Website:** http://dixielandcabins.com/

LBL's Neville Bay:

This camp area is another of Land Between the Lake's many dispersed, backcountry campsites, and is also a favorite of the locals and tourists alike. While there are not very many level sites large enough for good RV parking, this is a great camp area for primitive tent camping.

Among the basic offerings of this camp, you'll find a nice picnic area, a boat ramp, and a vault toilet for public use.

Neville bay is a great area for swimming, boating, camping and kayaking. It can be a pretty popular spot in peak season, so plan ahead, show up early and have a back up plan in case the area is full, as this is also a first come, first serve campsite!

- **Address:** Neville Bay Road, Dover, TN 37058
- **Phone Number:** (270) 924-2000
- **Website:** https://landbetweenthelakes.us/seendo/camping/basic/

Turkey Bay: *(Note: TB is technically not in Stewart County, but is part of LBL and is worth mentioning as it is a SC local FAVORITE!)*

Ah, yes! The most exciting and thrilling bay in LBL! If you google this popular place on Google, you will find that this particular area has hands down more reviews than any other place in LBL. Turkey bay shows off online with an impressive 4.8/5 starts with over 300 reviews - and for good reason.

If you're into jeepin', 4 wheelin', or any other ATV / OHV activity, this area will only leave you wanting more!! These OHV trails range from EXTREME, to more gentle rides suited for kids. You'll never run out of beautiful scenery, and there's more riding trails here than you can get through in one day!

In addition to over 100 miles of fun riding trails, Turkey Bay is also an excellent camping and swimming spot, complete with access to drinking water, chemical toilets, a pavilion, and has two 24 hour generator areas, perfect for those camping in style!

IMPORTANT NOTE: Please view TB's website or call ahead for details and hours. A permit and waiver are required in order to use these trails!

Address: 80 Turkey Creek Road, Golden Pond, KY 42211
Phone Number: 270-924-2233
Website: https://landbetweenthelakes.us/seendo/trails/turkey-bay/

Parks

D*yer's Creek:*

This park is located on the left hand side, right before you hit the bridge going into the town of Dover.. It is a paved road that's fairly easy to find. Dyer's Creek park is extremely spacious, with plenty of room for people to enjoy the outdoors. It is situated on an edge of Lake Barkley, and is a popular place to take the boat or kayak out for the day.

The first parking lot you'll come to is fairly large, and is great for parking your trailers/boats. There is a fishing dock and a boat ramp located here. If you continue straight, beyond the metal park gate, you'll see the bathrooms on your left, and two additional areas for parking on your right. The main park with playground and pavilion is at the end of the road past the bathrooms.

This is a great family park, with several picnic tables and grills, a swingset, as well as a playground that is surrounded by sand, so make sure to bring those sand toys for the kids! This park has a large shaded pavilion that can be reserved ahead of time for big parties/events, and will hold up to 100 people. There is also a water spigot near the pavilion that can be used as needed. I have even seen people hook up a sprinkler to it for kids!

Dyer's creek can be a great place for people to take a dip in the lake, but be wary of the fact that many people also fish here, so it's a good idea to make sure everyone is wearing protective water shoes. In addition to fishing and swimming, there is also a volleyball net in a sanded area, and a large open grassy area for plenty of other activities. Bring a football or frisbee to toss around, and let the kids enjoy a game of tag!

- **Address:** Dyer Creek Boat Dock Road, Dover, TN 37058
- **Phone Number:** (270) 362-4236
- **Website:** https://www.recreation.gov/camping/campgrounds/232579

Lick Creek:

Located only a few miles from the heart of Dover, this park is leased from the U.S. Corp of Engineers, and is operated and maintained by the town of Dover. There are 52 acres on this property, giving plenty of room for a hiking trail, playground, pickleball court, basketball court, and more.

You can find boat parking space towards the end of the road near the water, and in this area you will also find the boat ramp, fishing dock, and an outdoor stage used for many events throughout the year. This is also another great place to bring your kayaks and other water toys.

Nearby this parking area you can also find the entrance of the ¾ mile, paved hiking trail. This trail, while somewhat short, is exceptionally enjoyable and comes with a breath-taking view. Following this scenic trail will take you through a few short patches of peaceful woods and then down by the lake for a good stretch. Along this trail there are a few strategically placed benches where you can take a seat for a moment or a few and enjoy looking out at the peaceful water! I highly recommend taking this walk around sundown, because the sunset's reflection in the lake is a marvel in itself.

Like our other local park, there is also a pavilion located near the playground area which is available to reserve for free by calling the number listed below. You are also invited to rent the stage down by the lake. Many fishing tournaments have been held at this park, and if you're interested in holding one there you can also do so by calling the listed contact number.

Lick Creek has a great playground set up, complete with a playset with slides, swing sets, a merry-go-round, and multiple spring riders for the littles! There is also a set of bathrooms near the playground, and a gazebo to hide from the summer sun!

A little something special that our townsfolk added to this park is a community box where people are welcomed to read the books, take the books, or even add books to the collection. It's a way to ensure every child has access to books, and is a beautiful way for people to share books with one another.

- **Address:** 398 Colson Road, Dover, TN 37058
- **Phone Number:** 931-232-5907
- **Website:** https://www.dovertn.com/parks_rec.html

Fort Donelson National Battlefield:

There are so many exciting things I could tell you about this National Park, which happens to be one of my personal go-to spots for enjoying nature, taking hikes through the woods, and back in my younger years (ha!) I also loved going down to the old rope swing with friends, where we would spend endless hours doing jumps off the bluffs at the water's edge.

Fort Donelson National Battlefield preserves Fort Donelson and Fort Heiman, two sites of the American Civil War. This 2000 acre park is rich in history and education, making all the scenic views, hiking trails, and wildlife presence quite the added bonus to the experience offered within.

A popular and highly recommended activity to do while visiting this national park is to take the six mile, self-guided driving tour. Discovering many areas to stop along the way, where you can check out signs with historic information, as well as many outdoor exhibits including the rifle pits, lower river battery, and earthworks along the Cumberland River. You will also get to see a statue that represents the veterans of the Confederate, many real life cannons, and even some reconstructed huts that depict the small homes the confederate soldiers lived in during the war.

Despite all of the rich history this national park holds, some might say the real stars of this park these days are Jack and Lizzy, the bald eagle couple who have taken up residence in the park for many years now. Photographers and hobbyists alike come to visit the park regularly, just to witness these eagle's magnificence in person, and if they're lucky, snap a few cool action shots!

"This pair of eagles came to Fort Donelson Battlefield in 2004, and began building a nest. Two eaglets were hatched the following year in 2005. Each year, they repair their nest and lay. In 2010 the first nest they built fell to the ground due to support branches dying and gave way. But that didn't hold back Jack & Lizzy. Later in the year they began to rebuild in a pine tree just left of where their old nest was. A group of photographers who gave themselves the title of Fort Donelson Eagle Photographers decided it was time to give these beautiful birds a name- and so became Jack & Lizzy. They were named after Jack & Elizabeth Hinson." -Connie Wilson (Photographer and huge fan of the Fort Donelson eagles)

Jack was a farmer in Stewart County, but more importantly a civil war Sniper. (You can find books about Jack Hinson in our public library.)

Over the years, Fort Donelson has become a fairly common place for physical activity, especially with the four different scenic trails to choose from: The Donelson Trail, the River Circle Trail, the Spur Trail to the Cemetery, and the Graves Battery to French's Battery Trail. Each of these trails is composed of dirt, rocks and tree roots, varying in length and in difficulty from moderate to more strenuous. It is important to note that none of these trails are wheelchair friendly.

You can find more information about these trails as well as on the rest of the park, on the NPS websites, or at the visitor center in town.

- **Address:** 120 Lock D Road, Dover, TN 37058
- **Phone Number:** 931-232-5706
- **Website:** https://www.nps.gov/fodo/index.htm

Cross Creeks National Wildlife Refuge:

Cross Creeks is a MUST on your bucket list if you're making a trip to Stewart County. Having been established in 1962, Cross Creeks Wildlife Refuge lies within the floodplain of the Cumberland River (now Barkley Lake). This extensively large refuge now spans a total of 8,862 acres, and is the safe haven for thousands upon thousands of wildlife in this area.

Some of the most popular activities to do in Cross Creeks include hunting, fishing, archery, biking, boating, hiking, horseback riding (BYOH), running, birding and photography. If you contact the refuge at least 2 weeks ahead of time, you can schedule a free ranger-guided program/tour for your family or group.

Many people like to come here for kayaking and canoeing, and there are 6 different hiking trails to choose from, varying from half a mile to 5.5 miles in length and varying in difficulty.

Cross Creeks conducts many educational programs throughout the year, and also offers a 10 mile, self-guided wildlife tour along the Southern bank of the Cumberland River. Definitely check out their website to find out all that you can do and see in this outdoors sanctuary! And please, consider making a type of donation to Cross Creeks, as wildlife conservation is SO very important.

- **Address:** 643 Wildlife RoadDover,TN37058
  Phone Number: 931-232-7477
  Website: https://www.fws.gov/refuge/cross-creeks

Boat Ramps/Swimming Holes

G*ray's Landing:*

Right before you would access the Ned McWherter (AKA Paris Landing) Bridge coming from downtown Dover, is a road off to your right that will take you down to Gray's Landing. This particular spot is a go-to area to watch the 4th of July fireworks over the lake every year for us locals, and the rest of the year it is typically a chill spot to launch your boats and kayaks, go fishing, or possibly go swimming with water shoes on! There are roughly 10 spaces for parking, and a small picnic area available as well.

NOTE: This area is NOT for camping!

- **Body of water:** Kentucky Lake
- **Location:** Forest Service Road, HWY 79, Dover, TN 37058

Hickman Creek Recreation Area:

Nothing fancy here, but locals describe this place as having a "very nice ramp" for launching boats, plenty of parking space, and also a nice place to have a picnic! Hickman creek boat ramp is also considered a local swimming hole, especially for teens and young adults.

Fun fact: If you jump in the water and swim almost directly across the lake to the other side, you'll find yourself at Fort Donelson's rope swing, a popular swimming spot within the teenage and young adult crowd.

- **Body of Water: Lake Barkley**
- **Location:** Lake Road, Dover, TN 37058

Blue Creek:

This secluded boat ramp/recreation area can be found by taking hwy 79 towards Dover, turning on Bumpus Mills road right before the bridge, and then taking a left onto River road.

Making the drive to this particular boat ramp in the spring and summertime is an exceptionally beautiful journey, with so many wildflowers, ponds, marsh and glimpses of the lake along the way! It's almost a guarantee that you'll encounter some sort of wildlife by the time you make it to the ramp!

Note: This is a gravel road, so take it slow!

- **Body of Water:** Lake Barkley
- **Location:** 205 Lewis Circle, Dover, TN 37058

Saline Creek Public Use Area:

Saline Creek has been my family's go-to lake spot since I was a young child. Tucked away at the end of Hargis Road in the very small town of Bumpus Mills, this area is very rarely "busy", and is actually mostly just used by boat owners to launch their boats. It is an extremely secluded boat ramp with hardly any traffic, but comes with an amazing view and plenty of areas to set up camp for the day to enjoy swimming at the boat ramp, grilling with your own brought in grill, and just relaxing or fishing near the water all day.

Sunsets over the lake here are stunning, and highly recommended! If you're looking for some place to be alone with nature, or enjoy the lake with your group without a high probability of being in a crowd, this an excellent choice of "public use areas", with a peaceful drive down a long gravel road, and plenty of nature to enjoy along the way!

Note: This area is managed by the U.S. Corps of Engineers.

- **Body of Water:** Lake Barkley
- **Location:** End of Hargis Road, Bumpus Mills, TN 37028

Bellwood Landing Boat Launch:

The drive into the Bellwood area will not disappoint. By the time you hit Cub Creek area, you will all but totally be surrounded by woods, getting to experience the serene and peaceful drive that often has views of the rushing creek as you make your way down to the Bellwood Landing boat ramp. Much of the last several miles of your drive will be gravel, so drive with caution, but do enjoy the views along the way.

The Bellwood area actually used to be its own little community, and is very rich in history. A few interesting pieces of the past remarkably remain somewhat intact and visible along your route.

Once you make it almost down to the lake, you will come across a large old house on the left up a hill that is fenced off, and will appear overgrown and in disrepair. While this may look like just some ordinary abandoned house, the original home owner of this home was Senator John Bell, who ran against Abraham Lincoln in 1860. John Bell was a slave owner, and local legend has it that this "Bellwood Mansion" is haunted by the slaves who once worked on this plantation. Unfortunately, nobody is allowed on this property, and it only became a fenced-in property after many years of local teens and young adults trespassing on the property as well as inside the house.

Not very far down the road, also on the left side, you will see the remnants of an old Iron Furnace that was once owned by John Bell. This particular iron company was originally owned by Bell and a business partner (last name Yeatman), and as another interesting fact, when Yeatman died, John Bell went on to marry his business partner's widowed wife! (Weird!)

And what would appear just a quiet, lonely little boat ramp in the middle of nowhere these days, was once a bustling little area where iron, along with many other goods, were transported down the Cumberland River.

The Bellwood boat ramp is fairly secluded, peaceful, and doesn't see a lot of traffic. This has been another prime location for swimming and launching boats over the years.

- **Body of Water:** Cumberland River
- **Location:** Bellwood Landing Road, Indian Mound, TN 37079

Conclusion

Bottom line here... Whether you're a history buff interested in learning more, an avid outdoorsman looking for adventure, or simply a busy person who needs to get away, connect with nature and disconnect from all the day-to-day responsibilities, you're bound to find your happiness in our quaint, historic little Stewart County. The southern hospitality doesn't get any better than the folks you'll find at our local campgrounds and resorts, and no matter what outdoor activity you're into, I'm confident you can find a great place to enjoy right here!

Stewart County, TN is vast in space, yet relatively small in population, making it the perfect get-away with ample forests, waterways and rolling hills for all your outdoor recreational needs.

Welcome, y'all! Kick your shoes off and stay a while. :)

Resources

U.S. Forest Service. (n.d.). *Basic, Dispersed, and Self-Service Camping. Land Between the Lakes.* Retrieved February 7, 2023, from https://landbetweenthelakes.us/seendo/camping/basic/

Fort Donelson National Battlefield (U.S. National Park Service). (n.d.-b). https://www.nps.gov/fodo/index.htm

U.S. Forest Service. (n.d.). *Basic, Dispersed, and Self-Service Camping. Land Between the Lakes.* Retrieved February 7, 2023, from https://landbetweenthelakes.us/seendo/camping/basic/

Dixieland. (n.d.). *DIXIELAND.* http://dixielandcabins.com/index.html

Bumpus Mills, Barkley Lake. (n.d.). Recreation.gov. https://www.recreation.gov/camping/campgrounds/232537

U.S. Forest Service. (n.d.-b). *Piney Campground. Land Between the Lakes.* https://landbetweenthelakes.us/seendo/camping/piney-campground/

Bumpus Marina. (2023b, February 4). *Bumpus Marina on Lake Barkley.* https://bumpusmarina.com/

Elk Harbor Lakeside Campground. (n.d.). *Elk Harbor*. Elk Harbor. https://elkharbor.com/

Brownfield Riverside Resort & Miss Kay's Country Store | Dover, TN. (n.d.). https://www.brownfieldriversideresort.com/

Fat Daddy's Tiki Hut. (n.d.). *Fat Daddy's Lakeside Tiki Bar & Grill*. Fat Daddy's Tiki Hut. https://fatdaddysfun.com/

LBL WHISPERING PINES CAMPGROUND & CABINS. (n.d.). Tripadvisor. https://www.tripadvisor.com/Hotel_Review-g60808-d1050387-Reviews-LBL_Whispering_Pines_Campground_Cabins-Dover_Tennessee.html

Whispering Pines Dover, TN. (n.d.). Facebook. https://www.facebook.com/WhisperingPinesDoverTN/

Boat Ramps and Launches. (n.d.). Living the Toon Life. https://www.livingthetoonlife.com/tennessee—-boat-ramps-and-launches.html

Dyers Creek, Barkley Lake. (n.d.). Recreation.gov. https://www.recreation.gov/camping/campgrounds/232579

Town of Dover. (n.d.). *Lick Creek*. Dover, TN. https://www.dovertn.com/parks_rec.html

U.S. Fish & Wildlife Service. (n.d.). *Cross Creeks National Wildlife Refuge*. https://www.fws.gov/refuge/cross-creeks

Fort Donelson National Battlefield (U.S. National Park Service). (n.d.).

RESOURCES

https://www.nps.gov/fodo/index.htm

U.S. Forest Service. (n.d.). *Basic, Dispersed, and Self-Service Camping.* Land Between the Lakes. Retrieved February 7, 2023, from https://landbetweenthelakes.us/seendo/camping/basic/

Made in the USA
Columbia, SC
12 May 2023